Trains

New York City Subway

by Julie Murray

2

Dash!
LEVELED READERS
An Imprint of Abdo Zoom • abdobooks.com

Dash!
LEVELED READERS

Level 1 – Beginning
Short and simple sentences with familiar words or patterns for children who are beginning to understand how letters and sounds go together.

Level 2 – Emerging
Longer words and sentences with more complex language patterns for readers who are practicing common words and letter sounds.

Level 3 – Transitional
More developed language and vocabulary for readers who are becoming more independent.

THIS BOOK CONTAINS RECYCLED MATERIALS

abdobooks.com

Published by Abdo Zoom, a division of ABDO, PO Box 398166, Minneapolis, Minnesota 55439.

Printed in the United States of America, North Mankato, Minnesota.
102021
012022

Photo Credits: Alamy, Getty Images, iStock, Shutterstock
Production Contributors: Kenny Abdo, Jennie Forsberg, Grace Hansen, John Hansen
Design Contributors: Candice Keimig, Neil Klinepier, Victoria Bates

Library of Congress Control Number: 2021940204

Publisher's Cataloging in Publication Data

Names: Murray, Julie, author.
Title: New York City subway / by Julie Murray
Description: Minneapolis, Minnesota : Abdo Zoom, 2022 | Series: Trains | Includes online resources and index.
Identifiers: ISBN 9781098226749 (lib. bdg.) | ISBN 9781644947265 (pbk.) | ISBN 9781098227586 (ebook) | ISBN 9781098228002 (Read-to-Me ebook)
Subjects: LCSH: Subways--Juvenile literature. | New York (State)--New York--Juvenile literature. | Urban transportation--Juvenile literature. | Transportation--Juvenile literature. | Railroad travel--Juvenile literature.
Classification: DDC 388.42--dc23

Table of Contents

New York City Subway

The New York City Subway is a rapid transit **system**. It is in New York City, New York.

7
1635
C
Do not enter or cross tracks

L6
Do not hold
New York City Subway
MANHATTAN
BROOKLYN
STATEN ISLAND
not lean on door

6

It is run by the Metropolitan Transportation Authority. It is the largest transit **system** in the world!

The Subway Then & Now

William Barclay Parsons and his team planned the NYC Subway **system**. They oversaw the construction.

Workers had to dig through rock, sand, and soil to build the tunnels. It was a dangerous job.

The first 9.1 miles (14.6 km) of track opened on October 27, 1904. There were 26 stations.

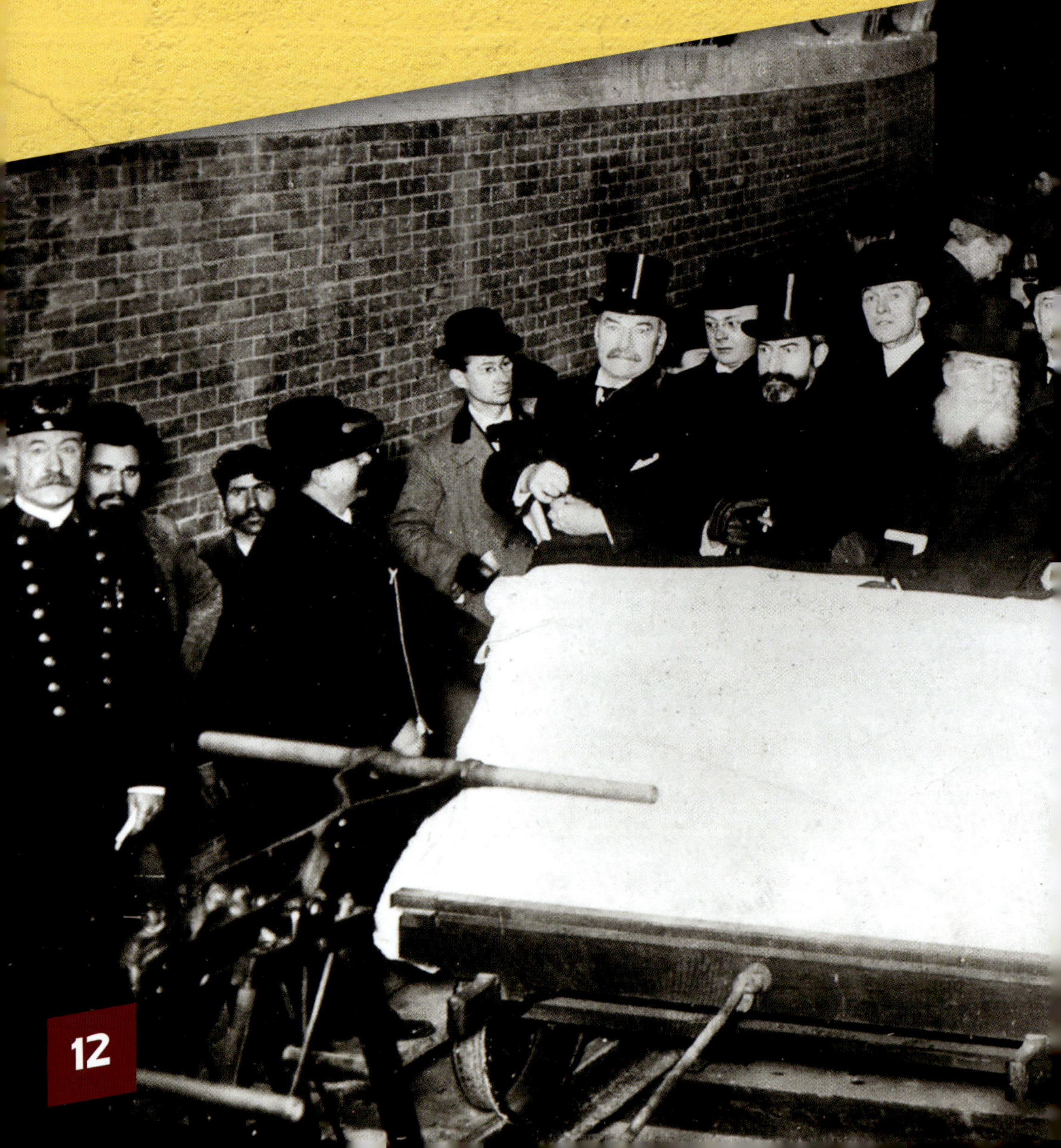

The subway runs on electricity. Power cables run in the tracks. These are connected to a power station.

1

Many **lines** have three or four tracks. These are for both **express** and local services.

Riders wait on **platforms**. The **cars** come every few minutes during busy times.

W4
E

Today, the **system** has 36 **lines** and 472 stations. It has more than 665 miles (1,070 km) of track.

7
7465
7464
7465
7464

More Facts

- The New York City Subway carries about 5.5 million people each day. That is more than 1.7 billion riders every year!

- In total, 40% of the NYC Subway runs above ground.

- It cost five cents to ride the NYC Subway in 1904. Today, a single subway ride costs $2.75.

Glossary

car – a vehicle that runs along rails, such as a railroad car or cable car.

express – a train that makes a small number of stops, usually major destinations, allowing faster service than local trains.

line – one of the many different lines, or railway, in a train system. Lines can be different sizes and serve different people. Some lines allow trains to move faster than others.

platform – a raised area next to railroad tracks for the boarding of trains.

system – a group of parts that work together as a whole.

Index

Online Resources

Booklinks
NONFICTION NETWORK
FREE! ONLINE NONFICTION RESOURCES

To learn more about the New York City Subway, please visit **abdobooklinks.com** or scan this QR code. These links are routinely monitored and updated to provide the most current information available.